THE SUPERFOOD
SMOOTHIE
RECIPE BOOK

**SUPER-NUTRITIOUS
HIGH-PROTEIN SMOOTHIES
TO LOSE WEIGHT,
BOOST METABOLISM
& INCREASE ENERGY**

Copyright © 2014 by Kasia Roberts, RN

Disclaimer

The information in this book is not to be used as medical advice. The recipes should be used in combination with guidance from your physician. Please consult your physician before beginning any diet. It is especially important for those with diabetes, and those on medications to consult with their physician before starting a diet.

All rights reserved. No part of this publication or the information in it may be quoted from or reproduced in any form by means such as printing, scanning, photocopying or otherwise without prior written permission of the copyright holder.

Disclaimer and Terms of Use: Effort has been made to ensure that the information in this book is accurate and complete, however, the author and the publisher do not warrant the accuracy of the information, text and graphics contained within the book due to the rapidly changing nature of science, research, known and unknown facts and internet. The Author and the publisher do not hold any responsibility for errors, omissions or contrary interpretation of the subject matter herein. This book is presented solely for motivational and informational purposes only.

Table of Contents

Introduction..4
Glycemic Index 6
Protein...8
Superfoods..8
The Single-Serve Package Method............................12
Post Workout Recovery..13
The Green Popeye..14
Strawberry-Raspberry Blast.......................................15
Banana-Coconut Breeze...16
Protein Boosters...17
Strawberry-Papaya Sunshine.....................................18
Mango & Peach Surprise..19
Apple-licious Banana n' Nuts.....................................20
Peach, Pear n' Pea Fusion..21
Fat Fighters & Metabolism Boosters..........................22
Mango-Lemon Shredder...23
Mango-Avocado Burner..24
Banana & Coconut Powerhouse 25
Blackcurrant-Blueberry Booster.................................26
Immunity Boosters...27
Berry, Manuka Honey and Walnut Fusion..................28
Beet, Apple and Cucumber...29
Spinach, Blueberries, Kale and Spirulina 30
Anti-Ageing & Cancer Protection................................31
Forever Young: Matcha Green Tea and Berries..........33
Spinach, Kale and Carrots..34
Beet, Banana, Raspberry and Carrot..........................35
Healthy Treats..36
Banana, Cocoa and Almonds.....................................37
Refresher: Avocado and Basil....................................38
Instant Bliss: Dark Chocolate and Cherry 39
Conclusion..40

Introduction

Most traditional breakfast options present undesirable nutritional profiles: fried eggs with bacon, toast with peanut butter, cereal with milk... Sounds familiar? I know I love the smell of bacon frying in the morning too! However, there's a price to pay. These typical breakfasts can be high in saturated and trans fat and sodium. In addition, a traditional, cereal-based breakfast is likely to be low in protein, and high in sugars and other simple carbohydrates, giving it a high glycemic index (GI).

A high GI, low protein breakfast can lead to an early morning insulin spike and subsequent mid-morning slump, with associated feelings of hunger, fatigue and irritability. This is undesirable for overall health, weight-loss and productivity. A healthy smoothie loaded with superfoods is the perfect way to charge up for a productive morning!

Smoothies are also a great alternative for people whose dietary restrictions forbid traditional breakfast options based around breads, grains and milk such as for individuals who are diabetic, celiac, vegan or lactose intolerant. In addition, with a well-designed smoothie such as those found in this guide, it is easy to tailor a healthy breakfast to the demands and challenges of any given day, whether this be exercise, stress, inflammation, or illness.

Smoothies are not universally a healthy option. Simply blending your breakfast doesn't insure you've made a healthy choice! Smoothies high in sugars and fats can be just as bad as processed bread and sweetened breakfast cereals. Many common smoothie recipes fall into this trap by including fruit juices, sweetened yogurts, full cream milk, and processed honeys.

This book describes 21 gluten- and dairy-free, vegan smoothies with an optimal nutrition profile for the active and health conscious individual. These smoothies are tailored for specific purposes such as: protein boosters, fat fighters and metabolism boosters, post workout recovery, immune boosting, anti-ageing, cancer fighting and much more!

I hope you enjoy all the delicious smoothie recipes and kick-start your morning in a healthy nutritious way!

Kasia Roberts, RN

Glycemic Index

The glycemic index (GI) of food refers to the rate at which a food causes blood glucose (sugar) levels rise after eating. Simple carbohydrates, which are broken down easily, release sugars into the blood more rapidly. This can cause a rapid spike in blood glucose levels, followed by a rapid spike in insulin levels. High levels of insulin cause the body to store glucose as fat. This phenomenon is what contributes to the fatty liver syndrome, prevents weight loss and can lead to weight gain. Additionally, high levels of insulin may contribute to insulin resistance, a risk factor in type-II diabetes. The fall in blood glucose after an insulin spike can lead to feelings of fatigue and lethargy. Examples of foods with a very high GI include: white bread and pasta and traditional cereals such as Cheerios, Cornflakes and even Branflakes.

Low GI foods release their stored energy more slowly, providing for a milder increase in blood insulin levels and an even tapering off of blood glucose levels. This provides energy at a rate more consistent with the demands of ordinary activity, and facilitates the body's use of glucose stored in fatty tissues as an alternative energy source. Combined with daily exercise, lower levels of blood insulin can help with weight loss. The fruits used in this smoothie recipe book have a low to medium GI. Below is a list of fruits with a low GI. Be creative and feel free to make substitutions in the smoothies with your favorite fruits!

Low GI Fruits

Cherries
Plums
Grapefruit
Peaches
Apples
Pears
Grapes
Coconut
Coconut Milk
Kiwi Fruit
Oranges
Strawberries

Protein

Proteins are the essential building blocks of all human cells and are particularly important in muscle tissue. Dietary protein helps the body repair damaged cells and create new ones. Protein is found in a variety of foods, though the comparative richness of meat and dairy products in proteins presents special challenges for vegans and the lactose intolerant. This book describes a variety of high-protein foods to make it easier to include dietary protein in a vegan or dairy-free diet.

Superfoods

Superfoods are foods, which have an outsized nutritional value, a particularly rare or important nutrient, or have been shown to have a particularly beneficial effect on health. They may protect against ageing, boost immunity, assist with weight loss, or help the body's natural detoxification or healing, among many other benefits. The superfoods featured in the following list are staples of the smoothies in this guide and are listed here instead of after each individual smoothie. In addition, many of the smoothies in this guide are based around one or more superfoods.

Chia

Chia seeds are small white, brown, or black seeds from a flowering plant native to Mexico and Guatemala. The seeds have a wide variety of nutritional benefits and are essentially tasteless, making them compatible with any smoothie recipe. Chia seeds are high in fiber, manganese, calcium, and protein, and have no cholesterol.

They are also the richest plant source of omega 3 fatty acids, which improve brain health and protect against arthritis and heart disease. Omega 3 fatty acids are also great for weight loss, especially for reducing belly fat. According to recent studies, the molecules present in omega 3 fatty acids bind to special receptors on a cell and literally switch on a gene that speeds up your metabolism.

The gelatinous coating developed by chia seeds when soaked slows the rate of digestion and may reduce insulin resistance – associated with increased storage of belly fat and risk of diabetes. Chia seeds have been shown to improve blood pressure among diabetics and may reduce unhealthy triglyceride cholesterol.

To prepare chia seeds for blending, soak them in filtered water for at least 10 minutes. If refrigerated the soaked seeds will keep for up to 3 weeks. The seeds will absorb any liquid, so you could also soak them in almond milk or coconut water. Soaking gives the seeds the consistency of tapioca.

Hemp Seeds

Hemp seeds have a mild, nutty flavor comparable to pine nuts. They are an unobtrusive complement to a range of flavors, and work well in smoothies. They are extremely rich in protein, calcium, iron, zinc, magnesium, phosphorous, and antioxidants such as vitamin E. Hemp seeds also contain an omega-6 fatty acid called gamma linolenic acid or (GLA). GLA has beneficial anti-inflammatory effects, supports healthy hair and skin, and helps to improve cholesterol balance.

Coconut Water

Coconut water is a sweet, naturally occurring, liquid found inside green coconuts. It is an excellent source of electrolytes, such as potassium, essential for hydration. Coconut water also has a low glycemic index and is relatively lower in calories than comparably sweet sports drinks. Bottled coconut water is widely available, though some brands have significant quantities of added sugars.

Matcha Green Tea

Matcha is a powdered green tea made from high-quality, specially grown tealeaves. Unlike conventional green tea preparations, which only steep the leaves in hot or boiling water, Matcha provides the entire nutritional benefits available in the tealeaf. This makes Matcha a far better source of vitamins, minerals, amino acids, and antioxidants. Matcha contains a particularly potent class of antioxidants known as catechins, which counteract free radicals from UV radiation and environmental contaminants. This may prevent cell damage and may reduce the effects of ageing. Matcha also boosts the body's metabolism and contributes to weight loss.

Almond Milk

Almond milk is a high protein, low GI milk substitute made from almonds and water. It is completely lactose free and has a superior nutritional profile to other common milk substitutes such as rice milk, and soymilk.

To prepare almond milk soak 1 cup of raw almonds overnight in filtered water. Drain the almonds and place them in a blender with 3 cups of filtered water (feel free to add a vanilla bean or a few drops of vanilla essence for taste). Blend the mixture on high for 1 minute and strain through a cheesecloth. Store almond milk cold in a jar or bottle.

Almond milk is widely available in health food stores but many products are heavily sweetened. Consult the nutritional information on the packaging to select an unsweetened product.

The Single-Serve Package Method

Many of the following recipes call for less than a natural serving size of certain fruits and vegetables (e.g. half an apple). A useful strategy is to make batches of 2 or more servings of your favorite smoothie recipes in preparation for the coming week. Separate these out into Ziploc bags and store them in the freezer. Making smoothie becomes a simple matter of selecting the appropriate bag, adding the liquid base of the recipe, and blending.

POST WORKOUT RECOVERY

The Green Popeye

The ginger in this smoothie has anti-inflammatory effects, which will assist in your post-workout recovery. The coconut water provides much needed electrolytes to assist in rehydration. The hemp and chia seeds contain plenty of protein to facilitate muscle building and repair.

Makes 1 Serving (889g)

Ingredients
1 green apple (peeled and cored)
½ cup spinach (frozen)
½ cup coconut water
2 tablespoons hemp seeds
2 tablespoons chia seeds (soaked)
2cm piece of ginger (peeled, diced)

Directions
Combine ingredients in a blender and blend until smooth.

Nutrition Facts
Calories 260
Fat 10g
Dietary Fiber 17g
Carbohydrate 23g
Protein 11g

Strawberry-Raspberry Blast

The red fruits in this smoothie are full of vitamins A and C, while the red pepper and cayenne add capsaicin, a natural pain reliever and antibiotic. Also great for boosting metabolism and facilitating weight loss. The ginger works to reduce inflammation.

Makes 1 Serving (613g)

Ingredients
1 red capsicum (stem and seeds removed)
½ cup raspberries
½ cup strawberries
2 cm piece of ginger (peeled, diced)
2 cups coconut water
½ teaspoon cayenne pepper
2 tablespoons hemp seeds
½ cup of ice (optional)

Directions
Combine ingredients in a blender and blend on high for 1 minute or until smooth.

Nutrition Facts
Calories 288
Fat 10g
Dietary Fiber 17g
Carbohydrate 23g
Protein 11g

Banana-Coconut Breeze

This post-workout smoothie includes coconut water and banana for hydration, almond butter and hemp seeds for a high protein yield, and ginger for its anti-inflammatory properties. Bananas are a very good source of vitamin B6 and a good source of vitamin C, potassium, and manganese.

Makes 1 Serving (774g)

Ingredients
1 banana
2 cups coconut water
1 tablespoon almond butter
1 teaspoon cinnamon
1 tablespoon hemp seeds
2 cm piece of ginger (peeled, diced)
½ cup of ice (optional)

Directions
Combine ingredients in a blender and blend on high for 1 minute or until smooth.

Nutrition Facts
Calories 499
Fat 18g
Dietary Fiber 16g
Carbohydrate 40g
Protein 14g

PROTEIN BOOSTERS

Strawberry-Papaya Sunshine

Numbers alone don't give this smoothie due credit for its protein maximizing qualities. Papayas are rich in papain, an enzyme proven to help your body digest proteins, allowing it to maximize the protein yield from the flaxseed and chia. Papaya is also very high in fiber, and this smoothie alone provides 60% of the recommended daily intake of fiber.

Makes 1 Serving (512g)

Ingredients
1 cup papaya
½ cup strawberries
1 banana
1 cup almond milk
1 tablespoon flaxseed meal
1 tablespoon chia (soaked for ~10min)
½ cup of ice (optional)

Directions
Combine ingredients in a blender and blend on high for 1 minute or until smooth.

Nutrition Facts
Calories 352
Fat 6g
Dietary Fiber 15g
Carbohydrate 40g
Protein 14g

Mango & Peach Surprise

The combination of nuts and seeds in this smoothie make it dense in protein, good fats, and energy: everything you need to get through a busy, active morning.

Makes 1 Serving (694g)

Ingredients
½ cup mango (diced, frozen)
½ cup peach (diced, frozen)
¼ cup pumpkin seeds
¼ cup almonds
¼ cup hemp seeds
2 cups almond milk
½ teaspoon vanilla extract

Directions
Combine ingredients in a blender and blend on high for 1 minute or until smooth.

Nutrition Facts
Calories 469
Fat 31g
Dietary Fiber 9g
Carbohydrate 20g
Protein 17g

Apple-licious Banana n' Nuts

The relatively high fat content of this smoothie prevents it from being an everyday staple, but it could be an especially apt choice before an intense workout or in anticipation of a late lunch.

Makes 1 Serving (761g)

Ingredients
½ apple (peeled and diced)
1 banana
2 cups coconut milk
½ cup walnuts
½ cup macadamia
½ teaspoon nutmeg
½ teaspoon cinnamon
½ cup of ice (optional)

Directions
Combine ingredients in a blender and blend on high for 1 minute or until smooth.

Nutrition Facts
Calories 681
Fat 46g
Dietary Fiber 16g
Carbohydrate 40g
Protein 12g

Peach, Pear n' Pea Fusion

The humble green pea is packed with healthy protein and gives this smoothie an excellent ratio of protein to calories.

Makes 1 Serving (852g)

Ingredients
½ cup sweet peas (cooked and cooled)
½ cup peach (frozen)
½ cup pear (frozen)
2 mint leaves
2 tablespoons chia (soaked for ~10min)
1½ cups coconut water

Directions
Combine ingredients in a blender and blend on high for 1 minute or until smooth.

Nutrition Facts
Calories 403
Fat 6g
Dietary Fiber 26g
Carbohydrate 38g
Protein 18g

FAT FIGHTERS & METABOLISM BOOSTERS

Mango-Lemon Shredder

This is an extremely low calorie smoothie thanks to the honeydew melon, which is largely made up of water and air, and has a high fiber content. It is nonetheless very filling thanks to the high quantity of protein packed into the spirulina.

Lemons are amazing liver detoxifiers and also alkalize our body. They may seem acidic based on taste but in the process of being metabolized by the body, they actually alkalize our bodily fluids and tissues.
Maintaining the health of the liver is also imperative to the body's ability to digest and burn fat, since the liver is one of the organs responsible for these functions.

Makes 1 Serving (500g)

Ingredients
1½ cups melon (diced)
½ lemon (juiced)
1 cup mango (frozen)
1½ cups almond milk
1½ teaspoons spirulina powder

Directions
Combine ingredients in a blender and blend on high for 1 minute or until smooth.

Nutrition Facts
Calories 171
Fat 1g
Dietary Fiber 4g
Carbohydrate 39g
Protein 8g

Mango-Avocado Burner

The Matcha and jalapeno combine to boost your metabolic rate and accelerate fat burning while the chia works behind the scenes to reduce insulin resistance and increase your capacity to process the energy stored in fat. The avocado helps to cut the spiciness of the jalapeno and it's loaded with healthy Omega 9 fatty acids. Avocados speed the conversion of fat into energy and boost the rate of metabolism.

Makes 1 Serving (359g)

Ingredients
½ cup diced frozen mango
¼ small jalapeno chili (finely chopped)
2 cups Matcha tea
2 tablespoons chia seed (soaked)
½ avocado

Directions
Combine ingredients in a blender and blend on high for 1 minute or until smooth.

Nutrition Facts
Calories 359
Fat 20g
Dietary Fiber 17g
Sugars 28g
Protein 6g

Banana & Coconut Powerhouse

Bananas are filled with healthy fibers that help curb appetite and help the body burn fat. Coconut oil is rich in medium chain triglycerides (MCFAs), which increases the liver's rate of metabolism by up to 30 percent, according to various research studies.

Makes 1 Serving (640g)

Ingredients
1 banana (frozen)
1/3 of a cup of blueberries
1/3 of a cup of strawberries
1 tbsp. coconut oil (organic extra virgin)
1 cup almond milk
1 tablespoon hemp powder
1 tablespoon chia seeds

Directions
Combine ingredients in a blender and blend on high for 1 minute or until smooth.

Nutrition Facts
Calories 427
Fat 20g
Dietary Fiber 14g
Carbohydrate 23g
Protein 13g

Blackcurrant-Blueberry Booster

The effects of blackcurrants and blueberries have been clinically established.
Blueberries help battle body fat while decreasing the risk of cardiovascular disease and diabetes. The results are linked to a high percentage of antioxidants that rid the body of toxins that lead to weight gain and other health problems.

Makes 1 serving (854g)

Ingredients
1 cup blackcurrants
1 cup blueberries
1 banana
2 cups almond milk
1 tablespoon chia seeds
½ cup of ice (optional)

Directions
Combine ingredients in a blender and blend on high for 1 minute or until smooth.

Nutrition Facts
Calories 411
Fat 12g
Dietary Fiber 11g
Carbohydrate 17g
Protein 9g

IMMUNITY BOOSTERS

Berry, Manuka Honey and Walnut Fusion

The vitamin C in the berries, combined with the selenium and zinc in the Matcha tea will boost your immune system. Quality, raw Manuka honey has anti-bacterial properties and may help to eradicate cold-causing bacteria living in the back of your throat.

Makes 1 Serving (673g)

Ingredients
½ cup raspberries
½ cup blueberries
2 cups Matcha tea
½ cup walnuts
1 tsp Manuka honey
½ cup of ice (optional)

Directions
Combine ingredients in a blender and blend on high for 1 minute or until smooth.

Nutrition Facts
Calories 473
Fat 4g
Dietary Fiber 10g
Carbohydrate 16g
Protein 10g

Beet, Apple and Cucumber

Beets are an excellent source of folic acid, fiber, manganese and potassium. They have been shown to increase the number of white blood cells, responsible for detecting and eliminating abnormal cells. Beets also contribute to healthy digestion due to their high glutamine content.

Makes 1 Serving (702g)

Ingredients
1 beet (washed and juiced)
½ green apple (peeled, cored and diced)
½ cucumber
1 cup coconut water
1 cup ice cubes
1 lime (squeezed)
½ cup basil
2 cm ginger (peeled)
1 tablespoon hemp seeds

Directions
Combine ingredients in a blender and blend on high for 1 minute or until smooth.

Nutrition Facts
Calories 188
Fat 8g
Dietary Fiber 6g
Carbohydrate 14g
Protein 9g

Spinach, Blueberries, Kale and Spirulina

Spirulina is an algae superfood, rich in vitamins B, E, manganese, zinc, iron, selenium, and antioxidants. Spirulina is also one of the densest sources of protein available. Spirulina aids liver function, balances cholesterol, reduces inflammation, supports immunity and may assist with seasonal allergies.

Makes 1 Serving (720g)

Ingredients
1 ripe banana
½ cup blueberries (frozen)
½ cup spinach (frozen)
½ cup kale (washed, de-stemmed and cut into small chunks)
1 cup almond milk
1 tablespoon hemp seeds
1 tablespoon chia seeds
1 teaspoon spirulina powder

Directions
Combine ingredients in a blender and blend on high for 1 minute or until smooth.

Nutrition Facts
Calories 288
Fat 1g
Dietary Fiber 9g
Carbohydrate 42g
Protein 13g

ANTI-AGEING & CANCER PROTECTION

Kale, Apple and Matcha Green Tea

Kale is a detoxifying, cancer-fighting superfood. It's packed with fiber and sulfur, both great for detoxification and overall liver health. Powerful antioxidants, such as carotenoids and flavonoids, protect against cancers, as does the high level of vitamin K. Kale is also rich in vitamins A and C, calcium, and contains more iron per calorie than beef. This smoothie is low in calories, while still maintaining a respectable ratio of calories to protein.

Makes 1 Serving (648g)

Ingredients
½ cup frozen kale
½ green apple (peeled, cored and diced)
1 ½ teaspoons Matcha powder
2 cups coconut water
3 mint leaves
½ lime (squeezed)
2 teaspoons Spirulina powder

Directions
Combine ingredients in a blender and blend on high for 1 minute or until smooth.

Nutrition Facts
Calories 86
Calories from Fat 5
Dietary Fiber 4g
Carbohydrate 10g
Protein 12g

Forever Young: Matcha Green Tea and Berries

This high protein, low calorie, smoothie is loaded with antioxidants to protect against the damaging effects of environmental pollutants, UV radiation, and cellular respiration – otherwise known as ageing.

Makes 1 Serving (650g)

Ingredients
2 cups Matcha tea
½ cup blueberries
½ cup blackberries
2 tablespoons hemp seeds
½ cup of ice (optional)

Directions
Combine ingredients in a blender and blend on high for 1 minute or until smooth.

Nutrition Facts
Calories 247
Fat 14g
Dietary Fiber 7g
Carbohydrate 11g
Protein 13g

Spinach, Kale and Carrots

This smoothie supports the health benefits of kale with a pair of other great foods: carrots and spinach. Carrots have been shown to reduce cardiovascular disease in addition to their antioxidant effects. Moreover, the polyacetylenes falcarinol and falcarindiol found in carrots have been shown to help inhibit the growth of colon cancer cells. Spinach, too, is full of antioxidants and vitamin C. It has also been associated with a diminished risk of colon cancer.

Makes 1 Serving (613g)

Ingredients
½ cup frozen spinach
½ cup kale (washed, de-stemmed and cut into small chunks)
2 carrots (juiced)
1 banana
½ cup ice
2 teaspoons spirulina powder

Directions
Combine ingredients in a blender and blend on high for 1 minute or until smooth.

Nutrition Facts
Calories 185
Fat 1g
Dietary Fiber 9g
Carbohydrate 20g
Protein 16g

Beet, Banana, Raspberry and Carrot

The beets in this smoothie contain betacyanin, which may suppress the development of some types of cancer. This is in addition to their white blood cell-boosting effects.

Makes 1 Serving (637g)

Ingredients
2 beets (juiced)
1 banana
2 carrots (juiced)
1 cup almond milk
1 tablespoon hemp seeds
1 cup raspberries

Directions
Process the ingredients with juice in a blender at high speed or until smooth.

Nutrition Facts
Calories 344
Fat 11g
Dietary Fiber 12g
Carbohydrate 30g
Protein 11g

HEALTHY TREATS

Banana, Cocoa and Almonds

This is a healthy alternative to a traditional chocolate-banana smoothie. The almond milk adds protein, while the agave nectar provides a low-GI sweetness.

Makes 1 Serving (613g)

Ingredients

1 banana
2 cups almond milk
¼ cup cocoa powder
½ teaspoon nutmeg
½ teaspoon cinnamon
2 tablespoons chia seeds
2 teaspoons agave nectar
½ cup almonds (soaked)
½ cup of ice (optional)

Directions
Combine ingredients in a blender and blend on high for 1 minute or until smooth.

Nutrition Facts
Calories 280
Fat 18g
Dietary Fiber 7g
Carbohydrate 28g
Protein 9g

Refresher: Avocado and Basil

Avocados are one of the richest fruit sources of protein, containing all 18 essential amino acids. In addition, the amino acids and antioxidants in avocado support healthy hair and nails, and fight the effects of ageing.

Makes 1 Serving (577g)

Ingredients
1 avocado (peeled and cut into small pieces)
2 cups almond milk
1 lime (squeezed)
2 teaspoons agave nectar
1 tablespoon fresh basil (roughly chopped)
½ of ice (optional)

Directions
Combine ingredients in a blender and blend on high for 1 minute or until smooth.

Nutrition Facts
Calories 486
Dietary Fiber 19g
Carbohydrate 27g
Protein 8g

Instant Bliss: Dark Chocolate and Cherry

Though this smoothie may taste decadent but it packs a nutritional punch and has a respectable ratio of protein to sugars and fats.

Makes 1 Serving (790g)

Ingredients
2 tbsp raw cacao powder
50g quality dark chocolate (70%+ cocoa)
1 banana
2 cups almond milk
2 tsp almond butter
1 cup cherries (frozen)

Directions
Combine ingredients in a blender and blend on high for 1 minute or until smooth.

Nutrition Facts
Calories 377
Fat 16
Dietary Fiber 12g
Carbohydrate 21g
Protein 8g

Conclusion

Breakfast can be a difficult meal for anyone but especially for the gluten- and lactose-intolerant. While including enough dietary protein for a healthy and active lifestyle is a challenge for any busy person, a vegan or dairy-free diet makes this task even more challenging. The 21 breakfast smoothies described in this report are a great alternative to traditional breakfast options. In addition they make it easy to start the day with plenty of protein, without having to resort to processed protein supplements!

The smoothie approach to breakfast makes it easy to include healthy ingredients not usually featured in ordinary breakfasts. The recipes featured in this guide, organized by theme, make it easy to vary your breakfasts throughout the week, to better take advantage of the unique nutritional properties and strengths of each smoothie.

The single serve package method makes it easy to plan your week around your breakfast. Commit to 4 workouts in a week when you make 4 recovery smoothies on Sunday, and 4 protein boosters for your rest days. If you know a busy, stressful week is approaching, alternate between the 3 immunity-boosting smoothies to give your body the nutrition and support it needs to face each day.

The recipes included in this book also allow you to easily keep track of the nutritional content of your breakfast, and to fit breakfast into a balanced diet, while avoiding the temptation to have "just one more" bowl of granola or piece of toast.

Smoothies are also fast and portable. With a prepackaged smoothie and a travel cup you can be out the door and on the way to school or work in 5 minutes or less, without sacrificing good nutrition!

Thank You

Thank you for purchasing The Superfood Smoothie Recipe Book! I hope you enjoy the nutritious recipes. If this book helps you achieve success in your health and fitness goals, please be sure to post a review on Amazon.com.
Best of luck on your journey to good health!

Printed in Great Britain
by Amazon